I0077009

# Tout

By:
Gary Martin Hays
Adam Weart

Copyright © 2012 by Gary Martin Hays and Adam Weart. All Rights Reserved.

Published by We Published That, L.L.C., Duluth, Georgia

THE AUTHORITY ON™ is a trademark of We Published That, L.L.C.

The cover design on all THE AUTHORITY ON™ books is trade dress of We Published That, L.L.C. This trade dress design includes the red and beige banner across the front of a Greek building imposed upon a background that from top down includes horizontal stripes of black, white, medium blue, white, and black.

No part of this book may be copied, reproduced or used in any way without obtaining prior written consent by the Authors or Publisher.

TOUT™ is a trademark of Tout Industries, Inc.

Limit of Liability/Disclaimer of Warranty: While the publisher and authors have used their best efforts in preparing this book, they make no representations or warranties with respect to the accuracy or completeness of the contents of this book and specifically disclaim any implied warranties of merchantability or fitness for a particular purpose. No warranty may be created or extended by sales representatives or written sales materials. The advice and strategies contained herein may not be suitable for your situation. You should consult with a professional where appropriate. Neither the publisher nor author shall be liable for any loss of profit or any other commercial damages, including but not limited to special, incidental consequential, or other damages.

ISBN: 978-0-9885523-1-9

For more information, please write:
We Published That, L.L.C.
c/o Adam Weart
PO Box 956669
Duluth, GA 30095

# THANK YOU!!!

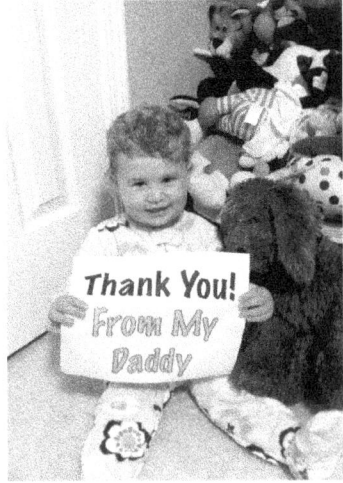

Seriously, we thank you for taking the time to purchase our book. We know that there are literally millions of choices available to our readers and we are honored that you chose ours to add to your library. We have one simple request to ask of you:

Please take a moment to REVIEW our book on Amazon.com. We would love to hear your thoughts on the content, as well as how you are putting our suggestions into practice. We sincerely appreciate your feedback. It is our desire to have this book become your main resource when using TOUT as a marketing tactic or for personal use. Any thoughts you have on how we can make our next version better will be greatly appreciated!

Thank you very, very much!

Gary Martin Hays and Adam Weart

# Table of Contents

# **Introduction**

Every day, the latest, greatest, "Next Big Thing" is being introduced in the world of social media. Most come and go and never gain any traction. Other sites, like Facebook.com and Twitter.com, have had lasting success and continue to thrive. Facebook has over 1 BILLION ACTIVE users as of October 2012.[1] More than half of these users are accessing the site with a mobile device.[2] Twitter has over 500 million active uses as of 2012, amassing an amazing 340 million tweets daily.[3] With Facebook having been launched in February 2004 and Twitter in July of 2006, these two sites are virtual dinosaurs in "social media years", yet they have had lasting success.

Facebook can attribute part of its continuing success to its ability to innovate. The website has recently spent a lot of money revamping the profile page to include a timeline which is more visual in nature. People are able to post photos and videos to the site, making it more engaging to people as they sit in front of a computer monitor or access the site on mobile devices.

Twitter's success can be linked to its simplicity. It is a quick and easy way to share instant messages with an audience that has previously raised their hand and said, "I want to know whenever you send a message." Links can be imbedded in the message so the audience can learn more.

And then along came Pinterest.com. From the time it launched in March 2010, Pinterest has become one of the top 10 largest social networks according to Hitwise data in December 2011.[4] It's easy to understand why this company has grown so rapidly. They have created a social networking site that allows its users to share photos and videos easily - either from a computer or a hand-held device. The visual revolution in social media has begun.

So what would happen if you could combine the interactive, social components of Facebook with the instant messaging/information sharing capabilities of Twitter, and bring in the visual components of Pinterest into one site?

Sounds like an amazing new social media site that is poised for explosive growth, doesn't it?

This book will introduce you to Tout™. In our opinion, this social media platform is not here to replace any of these other sites, but is a wonderful complement to a balanced social media strategy.

Read on to learn more about Tout, why you should use it, how to use it, and discover the best practices for Touting either personally or for your company!

# Tout

In less than 5 minutes, YOU can have something in common with the following people:

From the wide, wide world of sports:

- Shaquille O'Neil (Former NBA Super Star!)

Shaquille O'...
@Shaq  ♀ Tout HQ  ➕ Follow

*VERY QUOTATIOUS, I PERFORM RANDOM ACTS OF SHAQNESS*

- The San Francisco 49'ers
- The Pittsburgh Steelers
- James Harrison (4x NFL Pro Bowl linebacker for the Pittsburgh Steelers)
- Chris Fowler (ESPN Sportscaster)
- Erin Andrews (Sports Journalist)
- John Cena (WWE Superstar)

John Cena
@JohnCena  ➕ Follow
*The Official Tout Page of John Cena*

## And with those in the entertainment field:

- Kelly Ripa and Michael Strahan

- Ryan Seacrest
- Dwayne Johnson (The Rock)
- Katie Couric
- Dolvett Quince (Trainer for "The Biggest Loser")
- World Wrestling Entertainment
- Lilian Garcia (WWE SmackDown Announcer)
- Bow Wow (Rapper / Actor)
- Fran Drescher
- Lisa Rinna

## Even Politics:

- Mitt Romney
- Paul Ryan
- C-Span

- 2012 Democratic National Convention

As well as Successful Small Business Professionals and Marketers:

- Amy Jo Martin
- Tracy Myers
- Chef Paul Flores
- FreeAndEasyTraveler.com

And Social Media Marketing Gurus:

- Gary Martin Hays
- Adam Weart

No clue?  Let's tell you a little more . . .

This "something" takes social media to a whole new level. With this incredible new "tool", you can have "15 Seconds Of Fame" over and over again!

Still don't know?

This new social media platform allows you to share instant messages and information with your family and friends - your audience of viewers - by using video!

Sounds expensive, doesn't it? Well it is absolutely FREE to use.

If it is not expensive, then it must be complicated. Right? Don't you have to shoot the video, set up a channel on one of the video hosting sites, copy the link, paste the link, and then send the link to friends?

No! It is incredibly easy to use!

Give up?

Four letters: Tout!

TOUT!

Never heard of it?

If you haven't heard of it, or even if you have but you still are not sure what Tout is, why you should use it, or how to use it, then you are about to learn!

Tout is positioned to take the social media world by storm. If they say a picture is worth a thousand words, how much is a 15 second video, available in an instant, sent to your "audience" worth to you (or your company or brand)?

Can't you just think of the limitless ways you can use this new App?

# Getting Started with Tout

## The Difference Between Tout and Other Video Social Networks

YouTube, Vimeo and Viddler are 3 examples of "Video Hosting" social networks that allow you to store your precious video content. Once stored, these videos can be easily searched and shared on the web.

Tout sets itself apart by only allowing you to record 15 seconds of content per video post, as well as allowing you to upload video directly from your smart phone. Trends in the current social ecosystem show that consumers desire smaller, more digestible, snippets of data, especially early on in new social connections. Twitter's popularity proves that people's attention spans are very short when it comes to new information... and really just about everything for that matter.

To illustrate the consumer's "short attention span", look no further than the news coverage of presidential races. During the '68 presidential election, the average political sound bite played on the news was 43 seconds. Today, the average is only 8 seconds. [1]

The lesson we should all learn from this –
especially when marketing our services through
social media channels – is to use the KISS
principle:

**K**     Keep
**I**     It
**S**     Short and
**S**     Sweet!

## Tout Terminology:

- Tout – It's a verb and a noun. Tout is a video
  sharing social network. Tout, as a verb, is the
  act of publishing a new video.

- ReTout – Much like ReTweeting in Twitter,
  ReTouting is when you publish someone
  else's Tout on your feed.

- Follow – When you follow someone on Tout,
  their Touts show up in your feed.

- Keyword – When you use Tout's search feature, keywords help you find Touts that relate to your interests.

- Hashtag (#) – The # symbol, called a hashtag, is used to mark keywords or topics in a Tout. Hashtags make it easier for people to follow along with topics and people that they aren't already following.

- Reply – Tout allows you to directly reply to someone's Tout by using the "reply" function. Your reply is always tied to the original message.

- Share – The share feature allows you to share your Touts with your Twitter and Facebook networks as well as through text message and email.

- Flag – If you come across inappropriate material or people you can flag them to notify Tout administrators.

## Web and Mobile Versions

You can use Tout from your mobile phone by downloading the free application at the Itunes App Store or at the Android Marketplace (Not available on Blackberry) or directly from your computer using a web browser.

Links for Downloads can be found at *www.Tout.com or:*

Download on the App Store:
*http://bit.ly/AppStoreTout*

Download on Google Play:
*http://bit.ly/GooglePlayTout*

If you intend to Tout from your computer, you will need a web camera to record your own Tout videos installed in your computer or laptop.

## Setting Up an Account

You can use your Facebook or Twitter account to create a new Tout account (or create an account using your email address). We recommend using the Twitter connect function to insure that your Twitter username matches your Tout username.

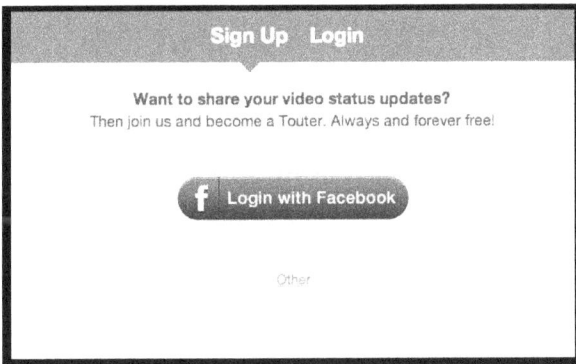

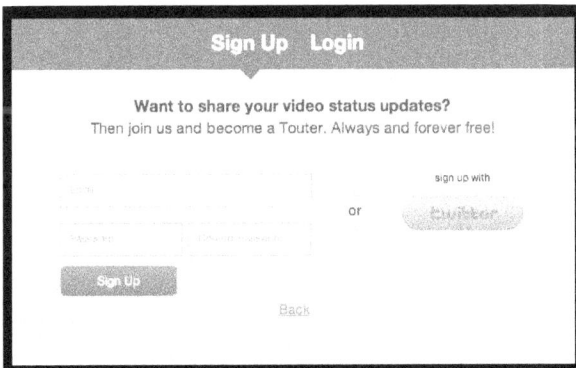

## Username Choice

If you have a Twitter account, use the same username on Tout as you do on Twitter to benefit from mentions. When you Tout and post on Twitter and someone replies, you will benefit from reciprocating username functionality.

## Update Your Profile

Upload a photo, modify your location, input your headline and provide a descriptive bio. Use a high-resolution photo that shows your professionalism. Tout limits the file size to 1MB.

If you are unsure how to resize images, we highly recommend a completely free resource for photo editing that is similar to Photoshop called Gimp. You can find the download for this program here: *http://www.gimp.org/*

Your Tout profile "Headline" can contain a maximum 255 characters so make the most of it by utilizing the top keywords associated with your business or profession. You can't use all of your keywords, so be sure and pick the best. Be brief and grab attention.

Headline Example:

AccuWeather    + Follow

@AccuWeather    ♀ State College, PA

*AccuWeather, established in 1962, is the World's Weather Authority. We provide local forecasts for everywhere in the United States and over two million locations worldwide.*

## Update Your Privacy Settings

Facebook Updates:  One setting on Tout allows you to auto-post to your Facebook page every time you watch a Tout. We HIGHLY recommend you DO NOT choose this option, as your Facebook friends may quickly get annoyed with your updates – especially if you watch a lot of Tout's at one time.

Update notifications:  This option enables you to select how you would like to be notified whenever there is activity on your account. What emails do you want to receive for activity on your account?

We suggest you limit your information overload by restricting the "activity" emails to a select few people. If you are mentioned or replied to in a Tout, an email alert will give you notice and opportunity to quickly respond.

## Follow Friends and Other Interesting Touters

You can use the search bar at the top of the page on the Tout website or phone app to find people or search by topics to locate people to follow.

We are both sports nuts and we follow a lot of the ESPN personalities. We also are "foodies" and follow our favorite restaurant, Gary's Bistro, and its celebrity Chef, Paul Flores. You could locate sports personalities like Skip Bayless by simply typing the word "sports" in the search bar as seen below.

## Search Box on the Tout Website:

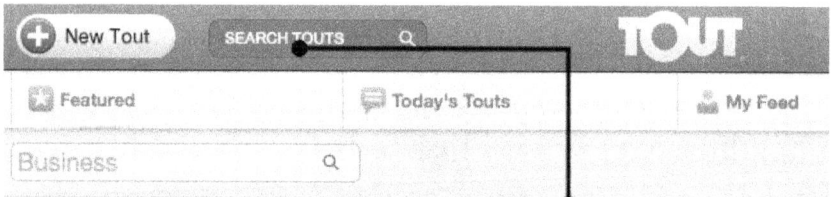

**Search**
Use this area to search for Touts that apply to your business or names of people you know

## Key Features (Mobile and Web)

Following Page: This is a page that shows you all of the people you are "following" or "watching."

Interactive Features include:

- Replies

- Retouts

- Shares

- Likes

Keyword, #Tag or Name Search: This is a form field that you fill in to search for topics or people of interest on Tout. It's like doing a Google search but it just searches the Tout network.

Trending Topics: The trending topics page shows you the most popular topics on the Tout network at any given time and the topics will change on a regular basis.

Website Widget: This allows you to customize a Tout video player that you can place on your website (more on this later).

# The Act of Touting

Here is a step-by-step guide on the actual act of touting, followed by photos to show how it looks on the web or on your phone:

1. Press the "Tout" button (alternately you can upload videos directly from your library).

2. If recording, Press the Blue "Tout" Button - you will have 15 seconds to record.

3. Watch the timer in the top right corner (counts down from 15).

4. Preview your video; re-record if necessary.

5. Write what is happening in the video.

   Use keywords and hashtags to help people find your Tout (more on this in future chapters).

6. Choose your "share" functions.

7. Choose whether your Tout will be public or private. Do you want this going to a select person or group, or do you want it published for all to see?

8. Press "submit" button when you are satisfied.

If you have chosen to share your video with different social networks, the video will immediately post to those networks.

## Screen Shots for the Web Browser (when you log on at Tout.com)

*Web Camera Configuration*

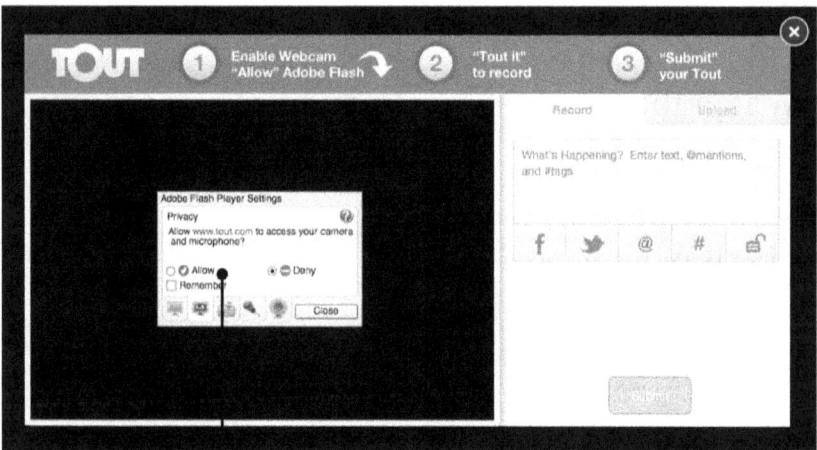

Fig 4.1

○ **Flash Settings**
Click the "Allow" option and also the "Remember" check box to give Tout permission to use your computer's camera

*Figure 4.1 - Web Camera Configuration: Click the "Allow" option and also the "Remember" check box to give Tout permission to use your computer's camera.*

## Web Tout Button

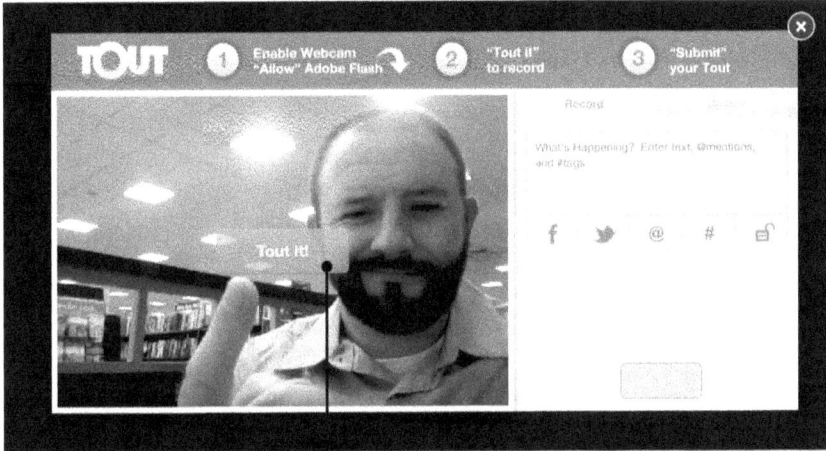

Fig 4.2

**Record Button**
Click the "Tout it!" button
to begin recording

*Figure 4.2 - Web Tout Button: Click the "Tout It" button to begin recording.*

## Recording Screen

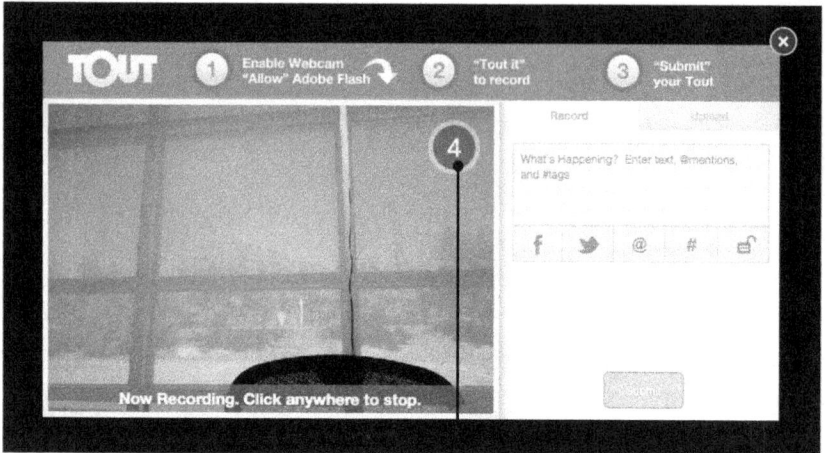

Fig 4.3

**Recording Timer**
This timer counts down
from 15 and the numbers
turn red from 3 down to 1

*Figure 4.3 - Recording Screen: The timer shown below counts down from 15 seconds and the numbers will turn red from 3 down to 1.*

# Tout Preview & Sharing Features

**Upload**
You have the option to
upload your own videos
from your computer

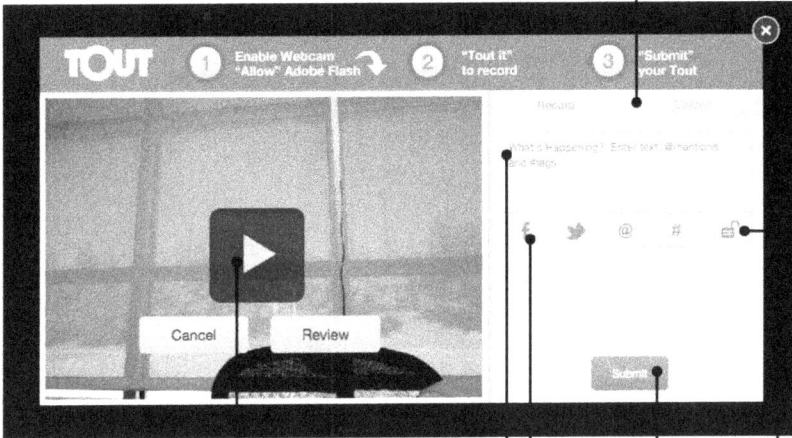

*Fig 4.4*

**Review**
You can review your
video before you
decide to submit it
by clicking the "Review"
button or the "Play" button

**Text Content**
The text box area allows
you to describe your
video and mention
other Touters

**Submit**
The "Submit" button
posts your Tout to
your account

**Share Buttons**
Choose between the
four share features:
Twitter, Facebook,
Text and Email

**Public Touts**
Choose between public
and private Touts - the
"Lock" button keeps
your Tout private

*Figure 4.4 - Tout Preview & Sharing Features: You can review your
Tout, add text content, change your share features and other settings
before you submit.*

## Screen Shots for Smart Phone Interface
# *Home Page Layout*

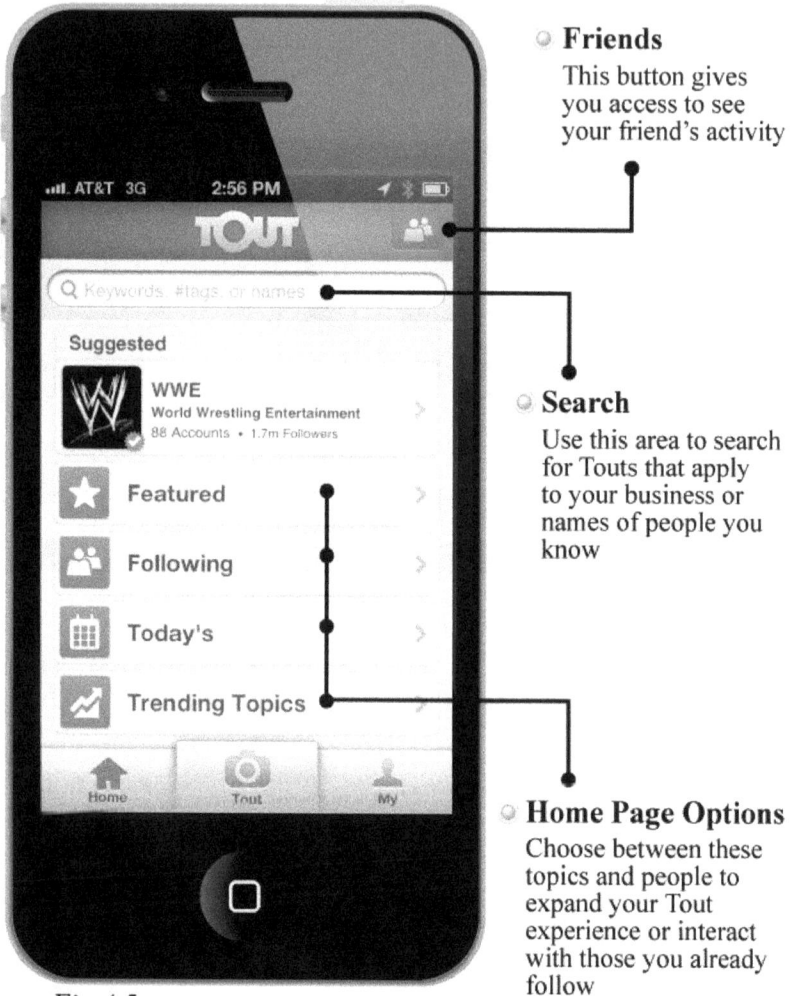

**Friends**
This button gives you access to see your friend's activity

**Search**
Use this area to search for Touts that apply to your business or names of people you know

**Home Page Options**
Choose between these topics and people to expand your Tout experience or interact with those you already follow

*Fig 4.5*

*Figure 4.5 - Home Page Layout: This page gives you access to friends, the ability to search, as well as some recommended Tout videos and accounts. The button at the button of this screen labeled "Tout" with an image of a camera is what you press to enable your phone's video camera to begin recording.*

## *Shooting Tout Videos – Screen 1*

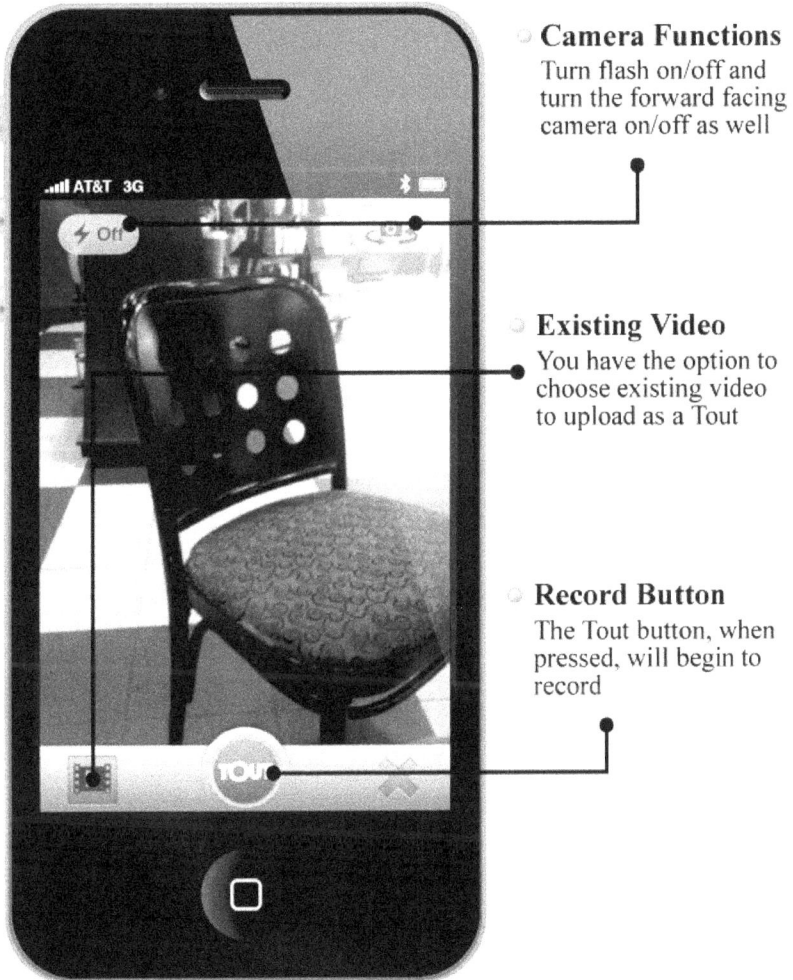

**Camera Functions**
Turn flash on/off and turn the forward facing camera on/off as well

**Existing Video**
You have the option to choose existing video to upload as a Tout

**Record Button**
The Tout button, when pressed, will begin to record

*Fig 4.6*

*Figure 4.6 - Shooting Tout Videos (Screen 1): On this screen you can change camera functions or upload existing videos from your phone.*

## *Shooting Tout Videos – Screen 2*

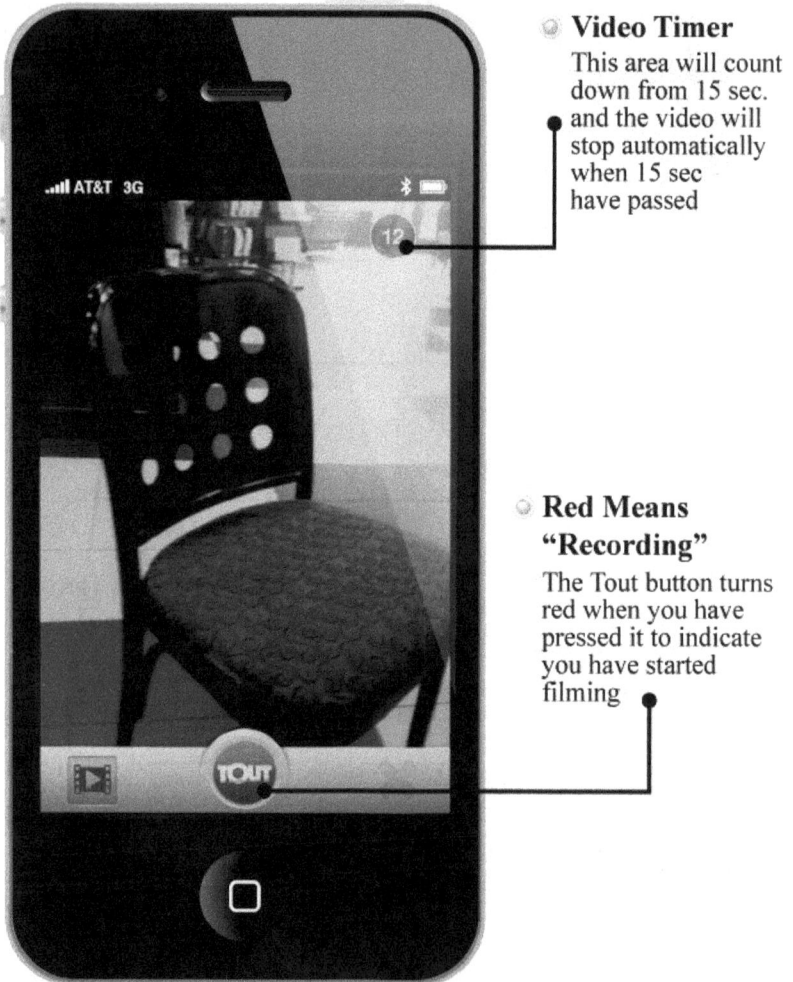

**Video Timer**

This area will count down from 15 sec. and the video will stop automatically when 15 sec have passed

**Red Means "Recording"**

The Tout button turns red when you have pressed it to indicate you have started filming

*Fig 4.7*

*Figure 4.7 - Shooting Tout Videos (Screen 2): While filming, you can see a timer in the upper right corner of the screen that helps you in spacing your words out to fill the allotted time.*

## Tout Preview & Sharing Features

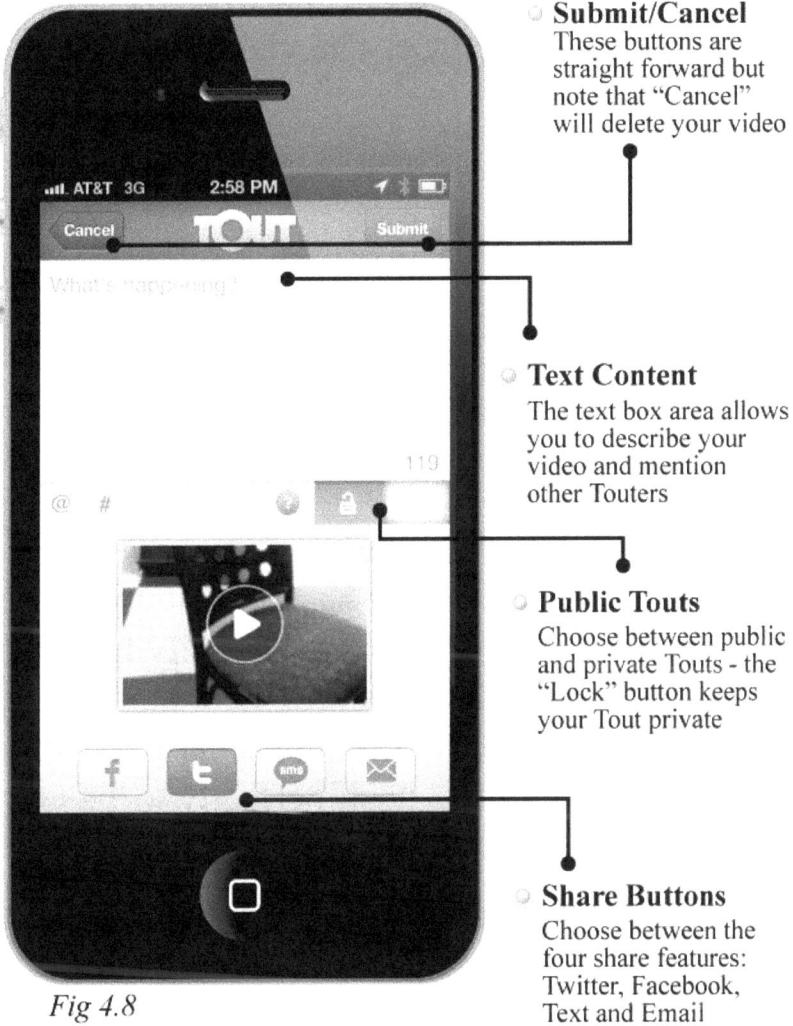

**Submit/Cancel**
These buttons are straight forward but note that "Cancel" will delete your video

**Text Content**
The text box area allows you to describe your video and mention other Touters

**Public Touts**
Choose between public and private Touts - the "Lock" button keeps your Tout private

**Share Buttons**
Choose between the four share features: Twitter, Facebook, Text and Email

*Fig 4.8*

*Figure 4.8 - Tout Preview & Sharing Features: You can review your Tout, add text content, and change your share features and other settings before you submit.*

## Where to Share

Tout gives you the ability to share your video content in various ways directly from the program's user interface. The video can be shared to:

- Twitter
- Facebook
- Email
- Text Message

## When & Why would you share to networks other than Tout?

**Twitter** - In our opinion, just about every one of your Touts can be shared on Twitter. Tout videos also can be played directly from the Twitter interface, making them more likely to be viewed. The ability to use hashtags (#) in your Touts lends itself perfectly to Twitter sharing and exposure.

New user interaction is driven by #s on Twitter because many users on Twitter utilize the # search feature to find new content relevant to their interests. Unless your Tout is uniquely purposed for another social network, all Touts are fair game for Twitter sharing.

****** *Special - Using Tout for Twitter Interaction - If you have an existing Twitter account with a decently interactive following, Tout is a great way to engage your Twitter followers with a video directed at them.*

**Facebook** - Opinions differ on the topic of Facebook over-sharing. We are in the boat of "fewer, more powerful shares on Facebook." Typically, one to two updates per day are reasonable on Facebook (especially for a business page). Share the single most useful content you create on Tout per day.

For example:  Chef Paul Flores at Gary's Bistro will often post a Tout showing the lunch special. He will send a Tout about the dinner special if it is different or if there is a special event that night at the restaurant. The point is he Tout's with a purpose. He does not Tout just to see himself Tout.

Note - Tout does not allow auto posting to Facebook Business Pages directly from their apps. You have to paste the link from the web app to your Facebook Business Page. The video player will be loaded in Facebook, so viewers can watch directly from their device.

**Email and Text Message** - These sharing features are a great way to introduce your content to people that are not typically involved with social networks. It would be best to only send texts and emails to clients/prospects that you know well. You can even send private Touts to people for a more personal touch. Private Touts are only viewable to the people that you send the link to via email or text.

But be very careful when doing this! Volumes could be written about the "wrong" or "inappropriate" messages being sent to the incorrect person or audience or a "private" message made "public."

# Tout Best Business Practices

## Define your users

Before we jump into some Tout specific business practices, let's take a step back and make sure that you have defined your business' users properly. A useful strategy for creating focused content is to define your buyers' personas; the persona(s) of key buyers of your company's products & services. A buyer persona can include demographic, firmographic, psychological and behavioral components of your buyers. Your user personas should define how you craft your content. Are they tech savvy? Are they under the age of 15? In other words, who is your typical customer?

In order to define your buyer personas, you should interview your customers to really define your typical "persona."

If you are new to a market or don't have many existing customers, you can interview prospects, referrals or even enlist web services to do the interviews for you.

## Be yourself - BUT be professional!

In the context of sharing content on your business social networks, it is important to remember that under most circumstances you should avoid profanity and extreme opinions. Be yourself but respect your community.

If you are a political pundit whose success is derived from extreme opinions and crassness, this rule does not necessarily apply to you. If you are a small business owner that sells software on the Internet, you can probably avoid putting your opinions out there in this forum.

## Provide desired content

One great way to find out what type of content people want is to research keywords that people are using most in your industry. One way to do this is use Google Adwords Keyword Search (*http://bit.ly/GoogleAdwordsTout*). The words that are searched for more frequently on the Internet in your area or industry are probably the most appropriate for you to use when creating content. Keywords are important to establish because when people search on Tout for topics that interest them, you will show up for the keywords that apply to you.

You can also search Tout for "Trending Topics" to see if you can offer fresh content to the conversations that people are most interested in following.

**Create a content matrix or editorial calendar**

A content matrix is created by choosing 5 keywords and placing them on the y-axis of a graph. Then choose 5 different types of content and place those on the x-axis. When you cross your keywords and your content ideas, you will quickly see how easy it is to come up with a wide range of content ideas based on keywords.

*We will cover specific content ideas later in this chapter.

## Content matrix example:

KEYWORD #5

KEYWORD #4

KEYWORD #3

KEYWORD #2

KEYWORD #1

TIPS/ADVICE    INTERVIEW    INDUSTRY NEWS    REVIEW    BEHIND THE SCENES

The reason you establish keywords to drive your content ideas is two-fold:

1. People search for Touts using keywords and you want people using your keywords to find you when they search
2. Your content will be focused and consistent when your Tout viewers start to follow you

Once you have created your content matrix and established your content ideas, plot them on a weekly calendar to help keep you organized. This content strategy can be used for blogging, Twitter & Facebook, as well as Tout. This content matrix will set your calendar for roughly one month (25 pieces of content)

## Consider placing a Tout widget on your website

As we discussed earlier, Tout empowers you to embed a Tout channel on your website or on a landing page using a framed application called a widget. You can choose which Touts show up. Populate your widget with Touts from users or hashtags that are applicable to your business or personal needs.

Example: Use the widget to ask a question on Tout and watch the replies populate in real time.

## Be patient, traction takes time!

It is very natural for social media efforts to take time & effort before real traction takes hold in a community.

## Keep interacting with like-minded Touters

The fastest way to expand you Tout community is to interact with new people that share your interests. Make every effort to reply to people that reply to you and even reply to new people when they Tout about topics that overlap your business interests. Your end goal should always be to help and share. Never sell your products in Touts or direct replies unless someone is specifically asking you to do so.

## Email useful Touts to your newsletter list

If you have a newsletter list that would benefit from updates about your business, using Tout as a video resource is a perfect accompaniment to your text and photo email updates.

## As your community grows, ask for interaction and input

In the early stages of your community growth on Tout, you should focus on providing useful content and less on asking for input or engagement. As your following increases and you become more comfortable with the Tout interface, you will feel more comfortable asking for input about your business products and services.

## 4 C's of Tout

1. <u>Content</u> - Provide useful information people want

2. <u>Creativity</u> - Don't post something you wouldn't watch

3. <u>Consistency</u> - Post consistently (1x per day)

4. <u>Connect</u> - Engage and respond to your community so they know you are listening


## Tout for Business (content ideas)

- Give advice/tips (avoid hard selling)
- Update your community on your daily business activities
- Quick Interview Series
- Ask for product reviews (reward your users in return)
- Highlight your employees
- Highlight clients' successes
- Ask for new product advice
- Video yourself quoting prominent industry leaders
- Show viewers your new products
- Film one part of the process:

- Example: Chef Paul Flores is the master of BBQ. He has a Tout on how he preps the Boston Butt he uses in his Pork Sliders. Chef Paul Flores takes his viewers into the kitchen to show them how he creates culinary magic. This truly adds to his "celebrity chef" status, but also makes him very approachable and human.
- Take the viewer behind the curtain, the counter, or into the kitchen. Give them an insider's view.
- Testimonial touts:
  - Bistro testimonials are great " influencers". It is compelling video to capture guests in their seats enjoying their food, drinks, and the atmosphere.
- Tout is a great way to promote a company's contest or sweepstakes.
- Live "TOUT" events.
  - Share what is happening to your clients/customers or those who will potentially do business with you. You can invite your customers to attend – in advance AND while your event is happening. Capture the moment and put it on TOUT.
- Promote new products and services using TOUT. Visuals help "Sell the Sizzle!"

- Highlight your company's success and achievements.
    - It shows you are growing, improving, and you are excited about your company and your company's customers.

## Tout for Personal Use
- Have fun
- "Mama Rule" - Don't Tout something if you would not want mama to see it
- Follow & Reply to like-minded Touters
- Search for Tags that apply to you and join in the conversation

# Examples of Businesses Using Tout

**Wall Street Journal** ® - World Stream
(*http://on.wsj.com/UkaCn7*)

The Wall Street Journal has empowered their worldwide journalists to add to the "WorldStream" - Their videos are streamed on one site from all over the world giving a snap shot of their news delivery in video format. Each journalist reports on topics ranging from world news to cooking and fashion to politics.

**World Wrestling Entertainment (WWE)** ® –
Early Adopters
(*http://on.mash.to/TF1w5N*)

WWE drastically increased the user base for Tout – Here are some eye opening statistics about WWE's effect on Tout[1]:

- The Tout app was downloaded more than 30,000 times for iOS and Android during and after *Monday Night Raw* (July 16, 2012).

- More than 400,000 people visited the app through Tout.com, mobile devices and *www.WWE.com.*
- More than a million Tout posts were viewed during and after the show, while more than 12,000 updates and replies were posted by users.

**Pittsburgh Steelers ® Contest** – #MyPGHSteelers (*http://bit.ly/SteelersTout*)

The Pittsburgh Steelers NFL team put on a video sharing team pride contest using the Tout platform as one way to submit entries.

Fans were asked to submit a Tout video stating what the Steelers meant to them using only 3 words. Winners were chosen and rewarded with game day tickets and merchandise gift cards.

**Self.com ® Teamed up with Jessica Alba** – Mom Knows Best (*http://bit.ly/SelfTout*)

Jessica Alba teamed up with Self.com to engage with social networks to learn the best advice that people received from their moms, using the #MomKnowsBest hashtag.

Overall, the ten-day campaign yielded 145,000 video views, as well as more than 3 and 5 million Twitter and Facebook impressions, respectively.

# 7 Typical On-Camera Blunders To Avoid

Let's face it - not everyone is ready to appear on camera every night as a "talking head" reading the news or providing juicy, entertainment tid-bits. But please understand - TOUT is not the nightly news and no one expects you to be a TV anchor. In fact, we think it is best if you don't try and act like a news professional.

We'll address some tips you can use to look better on camera later in this book, but we think it is very important to stress the mistakes you should not make first:

1. DO NOT talk just to talk.
   And don't just TOUT to TOUT. Have a single point for your message and do not ramble. 15 seconds will seem like an eternity to the viewer if you have not put any thought into your message. If you waste the viewer's time, they will be less likely to watch your next TOUT.

2. DO NOT look down at the camera!
   Always hold the camera (or whatever

smart phone or device you are using to film) at or above your eye level. Think about the viewer's perspective. They do not want to look up your nostrils or feel as though you are "looking down" on them!

3. DO NOT film into the light!

This will drastically effect the video quality. If you film with the light behind you, be careful that you don't have you or other people in the video squinting because they can't see either!

4. DO NOT start your video off talking to someone else!

For example, we have watched TOO many videos where the person that is being filmed (or that is filming themselves) says something like this on camera:

i. "OK, here we go" or "Camera rolling."

ii. Know when the camera is starting or have the videographer use a hand signal to let you know the camera is rolling.

5. DO NOT let your eyes wander all over the place when you start filming.

> Look into the camera like you are looking into the eyes of your audience. Know where the camera is before you start filming.

6. DO NOT speak in a lifeless, monotone voice or at such a low volume no one can hear you!

> Have some pep in your voice - and some energy when you are in front of the camera! You can have the greatest message ever placed in a 15 second video, but if your delivery is low energy, no one will care!

7. DO NOT look away from the camera until you KNOW it has stopped filming.

> When you have finished your message, hold your smile and keep looking at the camera for several seconds to make sure you have used the entire 15 seconds of video! You don't want to have the camera catch you looking away at the end or saying something and it only catches part of it.

# How Can You Make A Video Compelling In Only 15 Seconds?

We have given you 7 common mistakes to avoid while making your video. But what steps do you need to take to get the most out of your video? What should you be thinking about before you ever turn on your camera?

The MOST important thing to consider before you ever start filming is "the message." What is THE message you want to convey to your viewer? In 15 seconds, you really only have time to focus on ONE message. Trying to get too many points into one 15 second video is not a good idea as you will be forced to rush through the video. This will only allow you time to get 3 - 4 sentences into your video. Any more, and you will have to speed through your video like an experienced auctioneer.

Think of it from the viewer's perspective? Is what you are going to put on film in 15 seconds interesting and informative? If not, do you really need to film it? Don't make a video just because you have a camera. Make it with a purpose. Why should anybody want to pay attention to you and to your message? And why do you need video to communicate your message instead of text?

*So how do you start?*

1. Put on paper - in one sentence - the purpose of the video. What is your message? Keep it clean and simple. Don't use language or jargon that only a few people understand. Use plain English.

2. Once you know the purpose or message, then write out 3 or 4   phrases that help support it.

3. Review you list. Put them in order of importance. What is the best lead sentence?  Start with that, and incorporate the others into your message.

4. Now CLOCK yourself saying your message. You will want to say at a normal, conversational pace. Don't rush it, and don't go too slow. If it is over 15 seconds, think again. You have too much content. Don't try and squeeze it in. Time to revise. If it is close to 15 seconds and you think you have all the needed elements, then practice it again.

5. Once you are sure you can COMFORTABLY get your message across in the 15-second time span, then you are halfway there. The more you do this, the quicker you will get the hang of it and have that "internal clock" set at the 15 second time.

Practice. Experiment. Delete it if it's bad and do it again! It's only 15 seconds! You aren't destroying an hour's worth of film. Relax!

The other half of the equation is HOW you will deliver your message. Now you must think about ways to make your video visually compelling. Here are some things to consider when you film:

## Background

- What will your viewer see behind you? If you are filming yourself standing in front of a busy street, can the audience hear you? Will they be distracted by the constantly moving cars, or will they be paying attention to the kid in the stopped car making faces behind you? If your background is more interesting than you, then you may want to consider alternatives.

- Are you filming into the sun or a very strong light? If so, the quality of your video will not be good. The converse is equally true. Is there enough light to illuminate you? If not, time to move. If you are filming inside, it probably will not hurt to turn on several lights. Just do not have a light directly over you or the person you are filming because that can create some shadows on the person's head or face.

- Is there too much noise to be able to hear you? This is a very big concern, especially if you are just filming with a smartphone. If the sound is too low or just plain horrible, people will not watch your TOUT - period.

- Sometimes, the moment demands you just point the camera and start filming so you do not miss the event. Just try and keep the camera steady with as little jerky movements as possible. Do not pan the camera too fast - meaning film from left to right or right to left, or up and down - at too quick a pace. Slow and smooth is the key. You do not want to try and recreate the filming style used in the *Blair Witch* movies.

- And always have your smartphone with you and be quick to record those special moments that happen every day - even if it is something you will not be sharing with everyone else! If you let the opportunity pass you by, chances are, you may not have another shot at it.

- If you want to film while walking, please walk in a forward direction for your safety!

## Your Appearance

- Let's make sure we stress this point to you. YOU do not have to appear in the video to make it compelling. In fact, no one has to appear in it. You can have a good video of some scenery, event, or thing while you talk and tell the story.

- Be authentic and genuine! NO ONE will care if you are not a professional. Don't change your voice. Just be yourself!

- ENERGY on camera is so important. You will be surprised just how much the camera can suck the life out of you! Be energetic, but not over the top. It will make the content so much more interesting when the delivery is exciting. Finish a sentence with the same energy which you started it. Don't let your volume tone off at the end.

- Make sure you are close enough to the camera so the viewer can see your face. The exception is when you want to pan around because the background is more important than you.

- Stand up straight. No slouching. Arms should not be crossed. No "fake" smiles. Just be genuine! There is nothing wrong with using your hands to gesture in the video - just don't overdo it! Make sure your body language - from posture to facial expressions to hand gestures - is consistent with your message.

- One of the first things viewers will notice about your video - or perhaps THE first thing - is your appearance. Is your hair messy? Do you have spinach between the teeth?

- Eye contact is extremely important if you are trying to build credibility through your video. Don't turn your eyes away from the camera lens. If you do, you look shifty and you are missing an opportunity to connect with your viewer. Just imagine the lens as the face of a trusted friend and talk to it.

## Your Clothes

- We don't want to get too carried away, but what you wear is something to consider. Does your "look" fit your "message"? Are you dressed in shorts for a video about your business? It may work if you own a gym, but it might be out of line for a dentist.

- White shirts do tend to have a "washed out" look on camera. Patterns - especially checkerboard or pin stripes - can give the appearance they are moving or vibrating on camera.

## Your Camera

- This may sound obvious, but please make sure you know where the lens is on your camera or smartphone. Also, make sure it is pointing at your subject. Some phones will give you the option of recording yourself without having to turn the camera around. Just a simple touch of the screen will change the direction of the recording.

- DO NOT block the microphone on your camera. If you do cover it when recording, you will get NO sound or it will not be loud enough for the viewer to easily hear it.

# Bonus Content:
## Video Filming Tips & Tricks

**Smart Phone Videography**

*Lighting*
Lighting is critical regardless of what camera you decide to use. Don't film in the dark. Shoot outside in the sunlight or make sure the room you are shooting in is well lit. You can also use professional video lighting if your budget allows.

*Stable Video*
Make your best effort to mount your iPhone or keep it stationary. Using a tripod is your best bet.

There are some very affordable options for smart phones here:

*http://bit.ly/StableVidOne*

*http://bit.ly/StableVidTwo*

*http://bit.ly/StableVidThree*

*http://bit.ly/StableVidFour*

*Sound Quality*
Here are some microphones that won't break the bank while giving a powerful sound to accompany your great content:

*http://bit.ly/SoundOne*

*http://bit.ly/SoundTwo*

*Camera Lens*
Just because you're using your Smart Phone, doesn't mean you can't benefit from interesting lens techniques. Here are some great products that provide a bevy of lens options:

*http://bit.ly/LensOne*

**Tripod Tips and Tricks**

*Panning*
In photography and videography, panning refers to the rotation in a horizontal plane of a still camera or video camera. To achieve a nice panning effect, place a rubber band around your tripod handle and slowly pull the rubber band. As you come to a stop, you will notice a natural and gradual slow down as you focus on your subject matter.

*Tilting*

You may find yourself wanting to take advantage of tilting your shots from the ceiling down to level view. One technique to achieve a smooth tilt is to loosen the grip on your tripod just enough to allow the camera to slowly tilt down while filming.

*Dramatic Tilt Zoom*

A dramatic tilt zoom is a great way to bring an object into focus to draw attention to it. You achieve this effect by placing an object on a surface and tilting your tripod so that it is focused on the object. Then, tilt your tripod back up to almost level and then tilt back in while you are filming until your back to being focused.

# **Conclusion**

**Start Today!**

Download the Tout app, set up your account, and start creating your content strategy.

You will get better with each and every Tout – we promise!

Here are some key statistics about Video Marketing in 2012. [1]

- Online video viewers will reach 169.3 million in 2012.
- 53.5% of the population and 70.8% of Internet users (up 7.1% from 2011) will watch online video in 2012.
- Mobile video viewers will reach 54.6 million in 2012.
- Smartphone video viewers will reach 51.2 million in 2012.

# **Notes**

## **Chapter 1 – Introduction**

1. Ortutay, Barbara (October 4, 2012). http://www.usatoday.com/story/tech/2012/10/04/facebook-tops-1-billion-users/1612613/

2. Sengupta, Somini (May 13, 2012). "Facebook's Prospects May Rest on Trove of Data". (http://www.nytimes.com/2012/05/15/technology/facebook-needs-to-turn-into-investor-gold.html).

3. (http://www.mediabistro.com/alltwitter/500-million-registered-users_b18842).

4. Sloan, Paul (December 22, 2011). "Pinterest: Crazy growth lands it as a top 10 social site" (http://news.cnet.com/8301-1023_3-57347187-93/pinterest-crazy-growth-lands-it-as-top-10-social-site/?tag=mncol;txt).

## **Chapter 3 – Getting Started with Tout**

1. Craig Fehrman (Jan 2, 2011). http://www.boston.com/bostonglobe/ideas/articles/2011/01/02/the_incredible_shrinking_sound_bite/?page=full

## Chapter 6 – Examples of Businesses Using Tout

1. Sam Laird (July 17, 2012).
   http://mashable.com/2012/07/17/wwe-tout/

## Chapter 10 – Conclusion

1. eMarketer (Jan 5, 2012).
   (http://www.emarketer.com/Products/Explore/ReportList.aspx).

# About The Authors:

## About Gary

Gary Martin Hays is not only a successful lawyer, but is a nationally recognized safety advocate who works tirelessly to educate our families and children on issues ranging from bullying to internet safety to abduction prevention. He currently serves on the Board of Directors of the Elizabeth Smart Foundation. Gary has been seen on countless television stations, including CNN's Headline News, ABC, CBS, NBC and FOX affiliates. He has appeared on over 110 radio stations, including the Georgia News Network, discussing legal topics and providing safety tips to families. He hosts "Georgia Behind The Scenes" on the CW Atlanta TV Network and has been quoted in *USA Today*, *The Wall Street Journal*, and featured on over 250 online sites including *Yahoo News, Morningstar.com, CBS News's MoneyWatch.com*,

the *Boston Globe, The New York Daily News* and *The Miami Herald.*

He is also co-author of the best-selling books *"TRENDSETTERS - The World's Leading Experts Reveal Top Trends To Help You Achieve Health, Wealth and Success," "CHAMPIONS - Knockout Strategies For Health, Wealth and Success" "SOLD - The World's Leading Real Estate Experts Reveal The Secrets To Selling Your Home For Top Dollar In Record Time"* and *"Protect And Defend."*

Gary graduated from Emory University in 1986 with a B.A. degree in Political Science and a minor in Afro-American and African Studies. In 1989, he received his law degree from the Walter F. George School of Law of Mercer University, Macon, Georgia. His outstanding academic achievements landed him a position on Mercer's Law Review. He also served the school as Vice President of the Student Bar Association.

His legal accomplishments include being a member of the prestigious Multi Million Dollar Advocate's Forum, a society limited to those attorneys who have received a settlement or verdict of at least $2 Million Dollars. He has been recognized in *Atlanta Magazine* as one of Georgia's top workers' compensation lawyers. Gary frequently lectures to other attorneys in Georgia on continuing education topics. He has been recognized as one of the Top 100 Trial Lawyers in Georgia since 2007 by the American Trial Lawyers Association, and recognized by *Lawdragon* as one of the leading Plaintiffs' Lawyers in America. His firm specializes in personal injury, wrongful death, workers' compensation, and pharmaceutical claims. Since 1993, his firm has helped over 27,000 victims and their families recover over $235 Million dollars.

In 2008, Gary started the non-profit organization **Keep Georgia Safe** with the mission to provide safety education and crime prevention training in Georgia. Keep Georgia Safe has trained over 80 state and local law enforcement officers in CART (Child Abduction Response Teams) so our first responders will know what to do in the event a child is abducted in Georgia. Gary has completed Child Abduction Response Team training with the National AMBER Alert program through the U.S. Department of Justice and Fox Valley Technical College. He is a certified instructor in the radKIDS curriculum. His law firm has given away 1,000 bicycle helmets and 14 college scholarships.

To learn more about Gary Martin Hays, visit
www.GaryMartinHays.com.

To find out more about Keep Georgia Safe, please
visit www.KeepGeorgiaSafe.org

EDUCATION:
 1986:     Emory University, Atlanta, Georgia;
B.A. degree in Political Science, and a minor in
Afro-American and African Studies.
 1989:     J.D. from the Walter F. George School
of Law of Mercer University, Macon, Georgia;
Asst. Research Editor, Law Review; Vice President
of the Student Bar Association, recipient of the
Class of 1977 Scholarship Award.

Contact Information
**LAW OFFICES OF GARY MARTIN HAYS &
ASSOCIATES, P.C.**
3098 Breckinridge Boulevard, Duluth, GA 30096
Telephone: (770) 934-8000

## About Adam

Starting with a BS
in Industrial Design
and a Certificate in
Marketing from
Georgia Tech,
Adam Weart has
spent the past
decade providing
unmatched design
and services to
clients, specializing
in corporate branding, social media and web
design.

Adam spent four years running Design and
Engineering for HomeWaves while leading the
initiative for branding, marketing and sales. During
his leadership, HomeWaves achieved their
industry's most prestigious recognition by receiving
3 National CEDIA Awards.

Adam is a Best-Selling Author, Inbound Marketing
Certified Professional, has received the "Carnival
of Real Estate Blogging Honors," and has been an
instructor for various Continuing Education
Courses on Social Media and Technology in the
Real Estate Industry. He has also been featured on

over 100 online sites including *Yahoo News, CBS News' MoneyWatch.com, The Miami Herald and The San Francisco Chronicle.*

Adam continues to extend his leadership and marketing creativity by leveraging all aspects of Social Media Marketing and Web Usability Design as a key leader at the Law Offices of Gary Martin Hays & Associates, P.C.

EDUCATION:
 2004: Georgia Institute of Technology, Atlanta, Georgia; B.S. degree in Industrial Design, and a certificate in Marketing.

Contact Information:
**LAW OFFICES OF GARY MARTIN HAYS & ASSOCIATES, P.C.**
3098 Breckinridge Boulevard, Duluth, GA 30096
Telephone: (770) 934-8000

www.ingramcontent.com/pod-product-compliance
Lightning Source LLC
Chambersburg PA
CBHW060643210326
41520CB00010B/1714